FEARLESS CONNECTIONS

FEARLESS CONNECTIONS

BUILD POWERFUL RELATIONSHIPS TO THRIVE IN REAL ESTATE

Michael Del Prete

Copyright © 2024 by Arizona Real Estate Investors Association

All rights reserved.

ISBN: 9798343230703

Table of Contents

Introduction: The Power of Fearless Connections 1
Chapter 1: The Power of Connection 5
Chapter 2: Why Network with the Rising Stars? 9
Chapter 3: They're Hungry—Building with Driven People 15
Chapter 4: You Grow Together 19
Chapter 5: Master the Art of the Follow-Up 23
Chapter 6: Leveraging Online and Social Media for Real Estate Networking 27
Chapter 7: The Most Important Relationship of All 33
Chapter 8: Giving First – A Lifelong Lesson 37
Chapter 9: Power Listening: The Key to Building Lasting Relationships 41
Conclusion: How One Connection Led to AZREIA 49
Fearless Connections as a Framework 55
Your Next Step: The Call to Action 59
About the Author 63
About Arizona Real Estate Investors Association 65

Introduction: The Power of Fearless Connections

In real estate, success isn't just about numbers, properties, or even skill—it's about connections. But I'm not talking about the superficial kind of networking, where you collect business cards and never follow up. I'm talking about fearless connections—the kind of relationships built on trust, understanding, and a genuine desire to help others succeed.

Looking back on my journey, one thing is crystal clear: relationships are everything. From my first deal to taking over AZREIA, the largest real estate investor association in the country, every major milestone has come as a direct result of a connection. But not just any connection—a fearless one. A connection where I wasn't afraid to put myself out there, offer value without expecting anything in return, and trust that the process would unfold in ways I couldn't predict.

This book is about those kinds of connections. It's about how building authentic, lasting relationships can change the course of your career—and your life.

What Is a Fearless Connection?

A fearless connection goes beyond the typical handshake and small talk. It's about being open, genuine, and willing to give before you get. It's about finding ways to serve others, knowing that when you create value, the rewards will follow—often in unexpected ways.

When I think about fearless connections, one story comes to mind immediately. It's the story of how I met Stuart at an AZREIA meeting. We didn't just exchange numbers and walk away. We built a relationship based on mutual respect and a shared vision. Through that connection, I eventually met Alan Langston, the founder of AZREIA. Years later, that relationship led to me taking over the entire organization.

This book will show you how to cultivate those kinds of relationships in your own life—whether you're just starting out or you're a seasoned real estate investor. I'll share my journey and the lessons I've learned along the way, but more importantly, I'll show you how to apply these lessons to your business and personal life.

Why Networking Is More Than Just a Business Strategy

Let's get one thing clear: networking isn't just a tool to get more deals or grow your business—it's a philosophy. It's about how you interact with the world and the people in it. When you shift your mindset from transactional to relational, you unlock new opportunities you couldn't have imagined.

Too many people approach networking with a "What can I get out of this?" mentality. But when you focus on what you can give, everything changes. Fearless connections are built on generosity and service, not on immediate returns. And trust me, the returns come—sometimes in ways you could never predict.

Take my experience with Scott, who became my partner in the call center business. We didn't connect over a business pitch. It started with a relationship through a mutual friend, Aaron, and evolved into a collaboration that now has over 300 employees. This wasn't a quick win—it was the long game. And it started with a simple, fearless connection.

The Real Estate World Is Built on Relationships

Real estate is a people business. Yes, you need to know how to analyze deals, secure financing, and manage properties. But if you're not building relationships, you're missing the most important piece of the puzzle.

Think about it: every deal you've ever done, every partnership you've formed, every opportunity that's come your way—it all happened because of a relationship. Whether it's a mentor who guided you through your first deal, a lender who believed in your vision, or a fellow investor who shared a lead, real estate is built on the people you know and the trust you've earned.

What You'll Learn in This Book

Fearless Connections will show you how to:

- Build authentic, lasting relationships in real estate (and life).
- Network with intention and purpose, both online and offline.
- Position yourself as an expert and leader in your community.
- Leverage your connections to create opportunities that last.
- Give without expecting anything in return—and watch as the rewards flow back to you.

You'll hear stories from my personal journey, lessons from real estate deals, and insights from some of the most influential people I've met along the way. But more than that, you'll learn actionable strategies you can implement immediately to start building your own fearless connections.

The AZREIA Connection

One of the reasons I'm passionate about this topic is because I've seen firsthand how powerful a connected community can be. AZREIA is a perfect example. As the largest REIA in the country, we're more than just an association—we're a network of investors, mentors, partners, and friends. The connections I've made through AZREIA have shaped my career, and I'm committed to helping others do the same.

Throughout this book, you'll hear about the resources AZREIA offers—from monthly meetings and workshops to online tools and community forums. But more importantly, you'll learn how to leverage these resources to build your own network and take your real estate business to the next level.

A Final Word Before We Dive In

If there's one thing, I hope you take away from this book, it's this: don't be afraid to put yourself out there. Don't be afraid to offer value before you know what you'll get in return. Don't be afraid to make fearless connections.

This book is for real estate investors who are ready to take their networking—and their business—to the next level. Whether you're just starting out or looking to scale, the principles of fearless connections will help you grow your business, strengthen your relationships, and create opportunities that last a lifetime.

Now, let's dive in.

Chapter 1

The Power of Connection

In real estate, your success isn't determined by how many deals you close—it's about the relationships you build. I learned this the hard way, early in my career, when I almost lost $60,000 and a key property because I was focused on the next quick dollar.

It was just two years into my real estate journey, and I had recently quit my job. With a family to feed and bills piling up, I felt intense pressure to keep closing deals. My strategy? Wholesale as many contracts as possible. I was always chasing the next quick win.

Then, I came across a deal on Central and Camelback—a small, 700 sq. ft. house built in the 1930s with a squatter inside. It wasn't pretty, but I needed it to go through. My inspection period was ending, my earnest money was on the line, and none of my cash buyers were interested. I was stuck.

Desperate for a solution, I turned to AZREIA, hoping to find help. I attended a subgroup meeting, and there I reconnected with Dennis, an investor I had worked with in the past. I told him about the property, and to my surprise, he was interested. The next day, he visited the house and decided to buy it. I was relieved—my $5,000 assignment fee was secured, and I could move on to the next deal.

But then Dennis asked, "Do you want to own it?"

I was confused. I had only thought about flipping the contract, not owning the property. Dennis explained: "I'll buy it, renovate it, manage it, and you can own 25%. Plus, you'll still get your $5,000."

It was a game-changing moment. I had been so focused on the short-term win that I hadn't even considered long-term ownership. Thanks to Dennis, I didn't just get a quick payday—I gained equity in a property that paid off big. Over the next ten years, I earned passive income from that property. When we finally sold it, my 25% share turned into a $60,000 payday.

This experience taught me a crucial lesson: Be patient. Think long-term. And most importantly, leverage the knowledge and experience of others. If I hadn't shown up at that AZREIA meeting and reconnected with Dennis, I would have walked away with just $5,000 and missed out on a much larger opportunity.

Building Real Connections

The lesson here is clear: In real estate, relationships are everything. But what does that really mean?

Many investors get caught up in the transactional side of the business—how many contracts can I flip? How many properties can I close on? But what sets successful investors apart is their ability to build lasting connections. These are the relationships that don't just lead to deals; they create trust, long-term partnerships, and opportunities that go far beyond a quick win.

Think of it this way: deals come and go, but the people you connect with stay in your life and business for years. The investor you meet today could become your business partner tomorrow. The contractor you hire for a flip could introduce you to your next great deal. The mentor who helps you on your first deal could become a lifelong guide.

It's about more than just showing up at networking events and handing out business cards. It's about building real relationships—ones where trust and mutual benefit are at the core.

The Key to Success: Show Up

One of the most powerful things you can do as a real estate investor is to simply show up. Show up at meetings, events, and places where other investors gather. You never know who you'll meet or what opportunities will come your way, but you have to be present to seize them.

I learned this firsthand with Dennis, and I've seen it happen time and time again in my career. Many of my most successful deals didn't come from marketing campaigns or cold calls—they came from the people I met at AZREIA meetings, networking events, or even casual conversations over coffee. Every connection is a potential opportunity.

But to build those connections, you need to be intentional. You can't just show up, shake hands, and hope for the best. You have to be willing to invest time, offer help, and add value to the people you meet. The relationships you nurture today are the ones that will support you as you grow your real estate business.

Thinking Long-Term in a Short-Term World

Most new investors are focused on the next deal, the next contract, the next payday. It's easy to get caught up in that hustle—especially when bills are piling up, and you're under pressure to perform. I've been there.

But if you're only thinking short-term, you're missing out on the real opportunities. The most successful investors I know aren't just chasing today's deal. They're thinking five, ten, even twenty years down the road. They understand that wealth is built over time, and it's built through relationships.

The more you can shift your mindset from "How can I make money today?" to "How can I build lasting wealth through strong relationships?" the more successful you'll become.

Take Action: Start Building Your Network

Here's what I want you to do: take a look at your current network. Who are you connected with that you could build a deeper relationship with? Who in your local real estate community has potential but is still on the rise? Reach out to them. Offer help, share resources, and be someone they can count on.

Start attending local meetups or joining online groups where other real estate investors gather. Don't go in looking to close deals. Go in with the intention of meeting people, building relationships, and offering value. The deals will come naturally once you've built trust.

Conclusion: The Power of Connection

Real estate is about more than numbers, properties, or contracts—it's about people. The relationships you build will create opportunities that no marketing campaign ever could. So, focus on building real connections, showing up, and thinking long-term.

If I had stayed focused on the quick win, I would've walked away from that property with $5,000. But because I was open to a long-term relationship, I walked away with $60,000 and Dennis as a friend and mentor for life. That's the power of connection, and it's something you can't put a price on.

Chapter 2

Why Network with the Rising Stars?

Everyone wants to network with the big names—the ones who have already "made it." It's tempting to think that if you can just connect with the top players, everything will fall into place. But here's the real secret: the real opportunity lies in building relationships with people who are still on the rise. The ones who are grinding every day, hungry for success, and open to new opportunities. These are the relationships that will grow alongside you, and together, you'll achieve far more than you ever could by chasing established connections.

It's not about who they are now—it's about who they are becoming.

The Power of Rising Stars

Most people make the mistake of aiming for those who have already reached the top. They think, "If I could just get in with that top investor, they'll give me the keys to success." But that's rarely how it works. The truth is, the big names already have their established networks. They've built their inner circles and are often less accessible—not out of malice, but because their bandwidth is limited.

On the other hand, those who are still on the rise are motivated. They're eager to collaborate, learn, and grow. When you invest in these relationships early on, you're planting seeds that will grow into strong partnerships over time. As they rise, so do you—and the bond you build with them is stronger because you were there from the beginning.

Building with the hungry, ambitious, and determined people who are still pushing toward their dreams can lead to deep, lasting relationships. These aren't just transactional connections; they're partnerships built on trust, loyalty, and mutual growth.

My Lesson from the Music Industry

I first learned this lesson in the music industry, back when I was involved in concert promotions and worked with record labels in Phoenix. At the time, I was surrounded by artists and musicians, all grinding to make it big. I worked with a lot of talented people, but it was the relationships I built with the people behind the scenes that would later become invaluable.

I was working for Loud Records—a label that represented major acts like Wu-Tang Clan, Mobb Deep, and Big Pun. I frequently worked with interns and marketing reps who were just starting their careers and trying to get their foot in the door. We were all hustling, trying to make our mark.

One day, I asked a marketing rep at Loud Records to help a friend of mine from Phoenix who was moving to New York City. I wanted to see if they could help him get an internship. Without hesitation, the rep made it happen. That single act changed my friend's life. He never came back to Phoenix and went on to thrive in the music business.

But the real eye-opener came years later. One of the interns I worked with at Loud Records gradually climbed the ranks. I left the music business, and we lost touch. A few years ago, I found out that the intern had become the Vice President of Tidal, Jay-Z's streaming service. I had witnessed this person's rise, but because I didn't stay connected, I missed out on what could have been a valuable relationship. That's when it truly sank in—the importance of maintaining relationships with people who are on the rise.

Had I stayed in touch, who knows what kind of opportunities could have come from that relationship? The lesson was clear: always value the people you meet early on, because you never know where their journey will take them—or how it might intersect with yours in the future.

From Music to Real Estate: My Experience with Gary

Fast forward to my real estate career, and I saw this same principle play out again, this time with a friend named Gary. I met Gary through Dennis, who I mentioned in an earlier chapter. At the time, Gary was new to the real estate community, although he was already a successful entrepreneur in other industries. We clicked immediately, sharing resources and helping each other navigate the real estate market.

Gary quickly built a large rental portfolio, but his real passion was barbecuing. Over time, he became one of the top competitive barbecue chefs in the nation. My wife, son, and I often attended his cook-off events, supporting his passion while staying connected, even as he shifted his focus away from real estate.

Years later, when Gary was ready to start selling off some of his rental properties, he reached out to us. He knew we had the resources and experience to help him move his properties, and my wife, being an investor-friendly agent, was the perfect person to list them. Over the next year, we helped Gary sell several of his properties. Between assignment fees and commissions, we earned over $100,000—and that was just the beginning. Gary recently called us again, ready to sell two more of his rentals.

If I hadn't maintained that relationship with Gary, I would have missed out on those opportunities. But because we kept in touch, helped each other, and built a strong relationship early on, we both benefited when the time came.

The Lesson: Invest in People Who Are on the Rise

The key takeaway here is simple: don't just aim for the established players. Seek out those who are on the rise. Be the person who recognizes potential before it's fully realized. By investing in people early on—whether they're new investors, emerging entrepreneurs, or someone still finding their way—you're planting the seeds of future partnerships. And when they succeed, they'll remember who helped them along the way.

Actionable Advice: Building Relationships with Rising Stars

Here are three steps you can take today to start building relationships with rising stars in your network:

Identify Rising Stars: Take a look at your current network. Who are the people that show promise but haven't fully "made it" yet? They might be new investors, entrepreneurs, or people who are still growing. These are the individuals to invest your time and energy in.

Offer Help: Reach out to them—not because you expect something in return, but because you want to support their growth. It could be offering advice, sharing resources, or making an introduction that could help them. Giving without expecting anything back builds strong connections.

Nurture the Relationship: Relationships take time to grow. Stay connected with these rising stars, even if it's just checking in every now and then. As they grow, your relationship will too, and you'll both be better off for it.

Conclusion: Play the Long Game

Building relationships with rising stars is a long-term strategy. You might not see immediate returns, but over time, these connections will become some of the most valuable assets in your network. As they grow, so do the opportunities you create together. Stay open to the possibilities, and don't overlook the power of investing in people who are still on the rise.

Chapter 3

They're Hungry—Building with Driven People

The hunger for success is contagious. When you surround yourself with people who are still hustling to make it, their energy fuels your own ambitions. These people are relentless, creative, and always looking for opportunities. And when you connect with them, you share in that hunger—it pushes you to aim higher.

My Experience with a Driven Group

For most of my time as a wholesaler, I ran a small operation. My day-to-day consisted of working with a virtual assistant and an assistant, but I wasn't constantly surrounded by entrepreneurs. It's easy to get comfortable when business is running smoothly, but one thing I've always known is that I don't know it all. My natural curiosity kept pushing me forward, especially when I started wondering, "How can I make money while I sleep?"

The answer was raising private money.

To learn this, I joined a mastermind focused on raising money and creative finance strategies. Most of the members in the group had similar levels of investing experience, and we were all there for the same reason: to buy more rental properties using private capital. But being in that group impacted me in ways beyond learning new real estate strategies.

First, I had to overcome a mental hurdle—it wasn't a free Facebook group or some casual online community. This mastermind cost $20,000 to join, more money than I had ever paid for training. Making that investment taught me to trust the process, invest in myself, and believe in my ability to succeed.

Second, the energy in the group was contagious. Everyone was eager to learn and grow, and that kind of enthusiasm is powerful. It brought a sense of accountability too. When you're surrounded by people all working toward the same goal, you don't want to be the one who shows up every week with excuses. It pushes you to get your tasks done, stay on your toes, and keep progressing.

By purposely surrounding myself with driven, like-minded individuals, I didn't just learn new strategies that I still use and teach to this day—I also accomplished something huge because of that group.

How Hunger Led to Success: The Six-Plex Deal

One of the guys in the mastermind, Ryan, and I decided to grab coffee one day. As we were talking, he mentioned that he had rental properties in Mesa, Arizona. The wholesaler in me immediately kicked in, and I told him about a six-plex I was negotiating. The owner was firm on her asking price, and I had reached a standstill with the deal.

Ryan suggested we take a look at the property together, so we set up an appointment for the next day. After walking through the property and learning more about the seller's situation, we decided to offer a seller carry-back. Rather than trying to get the seller to lower her price, we agreed to her terms but structured the deal creatively. Ryan had a private lender who funded the down payment, holding costs, and renovations, meaning we had virtually no money out of pocket.

Here's how the deal worked: We purchased the property for $200,000, putting $25,000 down and carrying a $175,000 note. After completing the renovations and leasing the units, we refinanced a year later and borrowed $250,000, paying back the owner and the lender. I haven't set foot on that property since we bought it, and today it's worth $1.2 million.

This deal only happened because I surrounded myself with hungry, driven individuals. If I hadn't been part of that mastermind, if I hadn't been around Ryan, this deal would never have materialized.

The Lesson: Surround Yourself with Hunger

The key lesson here is that hunger is a powerful motivator. By aligning yourself with driven people who are still pushing to reach their goals, you tap into their energy and share in their enthusiasm. They'll push you to keep moving forward, even when you hit roadblocks.

Building relationships with these individuals not only opens doors to new deals and opportunities but also ensures that you keep growing alongside them.

Actionable Advice: Seek Out and Collaborate with Driven People

Find the Hungry People: Identify the individuals in your network who are still working hard to reach their goals. They might not be the most experienced investors yet, but their drive and determination make them valuable partners.

Work Together: Don't hesitate to collaborate with newer investors or entrepreneurs who are hungry for success. Their fresh perspectives and relentless drive can fuel your own progress.

Push Each Other: Join mastermind groups or accountability networks where everyone is striving for similar goals. The energy and motivation from these environments will push you to achieve more.

Conclusion: Energy Breeds Success

Success breeds success, but more importantly, hunger breeds success. When you surround yourself with ambitious people who are still working hard to achieve their dreams, that energy pushes you to reach higher. The relationships you build with driven individuals won't just help you close more deals—they'll inspire you to grow, adapt, and continually chase your own goals.

Expanded Concept of Hunger

In real estate, success often depends on your environment. If you surround yourself with people who have already "made it," their hunger may have diminished. But when you connect with those who are still on the rise, their energy and drive are infectious. These are the people willing to go the extra mile, think creatively to solve problems, and constantly look for opportunities. They bring that energy into their relationships, which in turn, pushes you to keep grinding.

Aligning yourself with these ambitious individuals is not just about doing deals or learning from them—it's about being inspired by their work ethic and determination. Hungry people will help you see opportunities you didn't notice and push you to achieve goals you may not have thought possible.

Chapter 4

You Grow Together

Success in real estate isn't just about individual achievements. When you grow alongside the people you network with, your collective success multiplies. Real estate is a collaborative industry, and when you build relationships with people on the same trajectory, you support each other, learn together, and reach new heights.

Growing with Elijah: My Life-Changing Connection

Sometimes, I pinch myself thinking about how things work out when you're intentional about putting yourself out there. Whether it's through networking or marketing, the connections you make can change your life forever. That's exactly what happened to me when I reconnected with Elijah.

At the time, I was working my 9-to-5 job at Verizon Wireless. During my 15-minute breaks, I would check voicemails from my wholesale marketing efforts. I was working on my second deal ever and had signs out advertising a "Cheap House for Sale." One day, I received a voicemail from a guy named Elijah. His voice sounded familiar, but I couldn't place it right away.

When I called him back, it turned out to be someone I went to high school with. We caught up, and during our conversation, Elijah mentioned that he had been wholesaling for five years. When he asked me what I was doing, I told him I was trying to learn the ropes of wholesaling. Right then and there, we both realized we were eager to grow in the same direction.

Elijah invited me to his office and, before hanging up, he said something that stuck with me: "Bring any lead that ever told you no." At the time, I didn't understand why he wanted the leads that had rejected me, but I figured, why not?

So, I met him at his office with a stack of 20 leads on paper—homeowners who had all declined my offers. We caught up, shared stories, and reconnected. He took those leads and committed to helping me. I also committed to visiting his office once a week, which became a routine I called "A Day in the Life." Over the next few months, I learned everything I could by observing him and absorbing the business.

Four months later, Elijah had turned those 20 leads into three wholesale deals. I had an extra $20,000 in my bank account, and my perspective on real estate had completely shifted. What I learned from Elijah was that he could "see the invisible." He knew I had negotiated incorrectly, priced the properties wrong, and made poor offers. He had the experience to know exactly where I had gone wrong, just like how you'd know the challenges of your job if you had to train someone new.

As we got to know each other, we realized our strengths and weaknesses. My background in the music industry had made me a strong marketer, and I was able to make the phone ring and bring homeowners to the table. Elijah, on the other hand, had five years of experience converting those opportunities into deals. I was generating leads, but he had the expertise to close them.

We quickly became 50/50 business partners, with Elijah also taking on the role of mentor. That first year in business together, I was able to quit my job at Verizon, and we completed 30 wholesale transactions. That connection with Elijah changed the course of my life forever. It taught me the value of joint ventures and mentorship—two powerful forces in real estate.

Growing Together Is Key

What Elijah and I experienced was the perfect example of growing together. We didn't just have complementary skill sets; we were both eager to learn, share, and grow. Our partnership wasn't based on short-term gains. It was built on mutual trust, shared goals, and a willingness to help each other succeed.

When you grow alongside someone else, your individual success amplifies. You push each other to do better, to learn more, and to reach goals you might not have been able to achieve on your own. The people you surround yourself with matter—especially in real estate, where so much is learned through experience and shared knowledge.

Lesson for the Reader: Grow Together, Succeed Together

The best connections in real estate are those where you both grow. Whether it's a mentor-mentee relationship, a business partnership, or just someone you meet at a networking event, when you invest in each other's success, your collective growth creates opportunities beyond what you could achieve alone.

Actionable Advice:

Start Growing with Others: Identify the people in your network who are eager to learn and grow. These are the individuals who will not only help you succeed but who will also grow alongside you.

Mentorship and Joint Ventures: Seek out mentors and look for opportunities to become a mentor yourself. Joint ventures can be a powerful way to combine strengths, share knowledge, and accomplish more than you could individually.

Check In Regularly: Growth doesn't happen overnight. Stay in touch with your key connections, check in on their progress, and offer your support. As you both grow, new opportunities will emerge.

Conclusion: The Power of Growing Together

Real estate success is not a solo journey. When you surround yourself with people who are on the same trajectory, you grow together. The connection I made with Elijah changed my life and set me on the path to success. By growing together, we both achieved more than we could have on our own. That's the power of intentional, collaborative growth.

Chapter 5

Master the Art of the Follow-Up

Early in my wholesaling career, I set my sights on a local investor named Sal. He was well-known in the area for closing large multifamily deals and had built a reputation as someone who only worked with established players. I had heard about him through the real estate community and knew that working with him could be a game-changer for my career.

But there was one problem: I was new to the wholesaling game, and Sal didn't think I had much to offer.

The First Meeting

I first approached Sal at an AZREIA networking event. He was standing in the corner of the room, casually talking to a few investors, and I saw my chance. With a deep breath, I introduced myself and mentioned that I was wholesaling properties in the area. He listened politely, but I could tell by his expression that he didn't see me as someone who could bring value to his business.

"Nice to meet you," Sal said, shaking my hand, "but I've got my own team handling deals like this."

I could feel the conversation slipping away, but I wasn't about to give up. Before the conversation ended, I asked if I could send him a few deals I was working on.

"Sure, send them over," he said, though it felt more like a courtesy than genuine interest.

Most people would have left it at that—a polite handshake, a brief exchange, and a quick move on to the next investor. But I knew that if I wanted to get Sal's attention, I'd have to follow up, again and again, proving that I had value to offer.

Persistence and Follow-Up

Over the next few weeks, I made it a point to follow up. I sent Sal a couple of deals that I thought might interest him. The first one? No response. The second? Nothing. Most people would have let it go, assumed he wasn't interested, and moved on to other leads. But I wasn't going to let this opportunity pass by.

I started showing up at the same local real estate meetings where I knew Sal would be. Every time, I made a point to greet him, remind him of the deals I had sent, and ask for feedback. I wasn't pushy—just consistent. Each time, Sal would acknowledge me, but I could tell I still hadn't earned his attention.

One day, I sent him a potential deal for a 10-unit multifamily property. The property was a bit rough around the edges—older, with deferred maintenance issues—but it had potential, especially for a seasoned investor like Sal. I sent him the details, expecting the usual silence.

But this time, he responded.

"Let's take a look," his email read. That was all I needed.

Turning the Connection into a Deal

We met the next day at the property. As we walked through the vacant units, I could see Sal evaluating the numbers in his head, sizing up the deal. I explained what I had found during my initial walkthrough, highlighting the potential rental income after renovations and the value-add opportunities.

Sal asked me pointed questions about the comps, renovation estimates, and projected cash flow. He didn't sugarcoat it—he wanted to know if I really understood the numbers and the potential risks.

In that moment, I knew my persistence was paying off. The follow-up emails, the casual conversations at meetups, the deals I had sent over—they had all laid the foundation for this moment. I had finally gotten his attention.

A few days later, Sal called me. He was ready to move forward and close the deal, offering me a $9,000 wholesale fee. That $9,000 might not have been the largest fee I'd ever made, but it represented something much bigger. I had finally earned the respect and trust of a major player in the real estate market—and it all came down to persistence and follow-up.

The Power of Follow-Up

That 10-unit deal became a turning point in my career. It wasn't just about the money; it was about building trust and a relationship with someone who initially didn't see my potential. The only reason I was able to turn that first cold introduction into a successful deal was because I followed up, again and again.

Following up isn't just about pestering someone or trying to get their attention. It's about showing that you're serious, reliable, and willing to put in the effort. It's about proving that you're here for the long game, not just a quick win.

In real estate, deals often come down to relationships. And those relationships are built through consistent, meaningful follow-up.

Lesson for the Reader

The key takeaway is that follow-up is where the real relationship-building happens. It's not just about persistence—it's about showing that you're genuinely interested in building a meaningful connection. Follow-up shows that you're reliable, invested, and serious about your work, which builds trust over time.

Actionable Advice

Follow Up Promptly: After meeting someone, follow up within 24-48 hours. A simple email or message acknowledging the conversation can keep the connection alive.

Stay Consistent: Create a routine for staying in touch with key contacts. Whether it's a quick check-in, sharing resources, or scheduling a catch-up, regular follow-up helps maintain the relationship.

Add Value: Every follow-up should provide value. Don't just check in without purpose—offer something helpful, whether it's advice, a connection, or an update.

Conclusion

Following up is where the real work in networking begins. It's how you turn introductions into partnerships and casual meetings into lifelong relationships. By mastering the art of the follow-up, you'll stand out from the crowd and build a network that's both reliable and full of opportunities.

Chapter 6

Leveraging Online and Social Media for Real Estate Networking

March 2020—a time the world will never forget. COVID-19 hit, and everything we thought we knew about our personal lives and businesses was turned upside down. Suddenly, we were facing uncertainty unlike anything we had ever experienced. There were no clear answers, no guidelines to show us how to move forward.

Amidst the health concerns for ourselves and our families, we still had to keep our businesses running. As entrepreneurs, we had no choice but to figure things out. The bills kept coming, employees still needed paychecks, and clients needed to be served.

On the real estate side of my business, even before COVID, we were already feeling the squeeze in Phoenix. Prices were rising, margins were shrinking, and positive cash flow was becoming harder to maintain. I knew it was time to explore other markets, so I began researching the Midwest as a potential area to invest in rental properties.

I settled on Cleveland, Ohio, for a few key reasons: the city's economic stability, the presence of five Fortune 500 companies, the Mayo Clinic, and steady job growth. My plan was simple—start by wholesaling in Cleveland to build new relationships and get familiar with the neighborhoods, regulations, and overall market. While my team and I learned the lay of the land, I would focus on building connections with sellers, cash buyers, and local wholesalers.

Social Media Comes Into Play

It was around February 2020 when social media became a key part of my Cleveland strategy. I received a call from Elijah, an old friend I mentioned earlier in the book. Elijah invited me to a comedy show with a couple of other real estate investors. One of them was Tony, also known as "Tony the Closer." If you're involved in the real estate world online, you've probably heard of him.

We hung out that night, talked shop, and made some great connections. After the show, Tony and I connected on social media, sharing each other's posts and building rapport online. That's when something interesting happened. I received a direct message from a gentleman named Xavier, based out of Cleveland, Ohio.

Xavier told me he saw me on Tony's Instagram story and wanted to connect if I ever planned on working in Cleveland. It felt like the stars were aligning because I had already been researching the Cleveland market for months and was preparing to start wholesaling virtually from Phoenix.

I messaged Xavier back, told him about my plans to wholesale in Cleveland, and suggested we hop on a call. We started talking, and almost immediately, a partnership formed. I had the marketing expertise and budget to get the phone ringing with motivated sellers, but I knew nothing about Cleveland's market dynamics. Xavier, on the other hand, was a local wholesaler with an established cash buyer list.

We decided to partner up and split everything 50-50. My role was to generate leads and bring deals to the table, while Xavier helped me understand the local neighborhoods, pricing, and comps. Once we locked up a deal, he would wholesale it to his buyers, and we'd split the profit.

Adapting During COVID-19

As the pandemic took hold, Phoenix's real estate market came to a halt. Everyone was unsure of what would happen next. Losing 10-20% on a $500,000 deal could mean a massive $50,000 loss, and investors were hesitant to take those risks. Meanwhile, Cleveland's market was moving full steam ahead. Properties there were more affordable, with average homes priced around $50,000. Even in a worst-case scenario, a loss would only be $5,000 to $10,000.

So, while Phoenix was slowing down, I was able to keep wholesaling from my kitchen table in Cleveland—during a global pandemic. Xavier and I built a steady pipeline, and I soon realized that Cleveland was filled with out-of-state and foreign investors, eager to buy properties in bulk.

That year, I completed 25 wholesale deals with Xavier and purchased 10 rental properties in Cleveland for my real estate business, all while the rest of the world was scrambling to figure out how to survive in the uncertain market.

The Power of Social Media

None of this would have been possible without the power of social media. If I hadn't maintained my long-term relationship with Elijah, I never would have gone to that comedy show. I wouldn't have met Tony the Closer, who shared my post on his Instagram story. And without that post, Xavier never would have seen me, and the connection that changed my business trajectory during COVID-19 wouldn't have happened.

At that moment, I realized just how powerful social media could be. A single post led to a partnership that helped me pivot during one of the most difficult times in my business career.

The Lesson: Use Social Media to Build Real Connections

Social media isn't just about posting content—it's about building relationships. By leveraging platforms like Instagram and LinkedIn, you can create real opportunities, even in times of uncertainty.

You never know who's watching, and a simple post can lead to connections that change everything.

Actionable Advice

Be Intentional with Your Content: Share posts that offer value—whether it's insights, tips, or behind-the-scenes looks at your deals. People notice when you're authentic and helpful. As part of AZREIA, we encourage you to check out our website at azreia.org, where you can join our online community and connect with like-minded investors.

Engage with Your Network: Don't just post and disappear. Engage with others on social media. Comment on their posts, share their content, and build real connections. Make sure to connect with AZREIA on all our social media platforms to stay in the loop and see how we foster engagement within our community.

Capitalize on Opportunities: When someone reaches out, don't hesitate to start a conversation. Social media is the first step, but turning those online relationships into real-life partnerships is where the magic happens. Start building your network today—join AZREIA's community at azreia.org, where you can take part in conversations and connect with experts and peers in the real estate industry.

Conclusion: Building a Real Estate Network in the Digital Age

Leveraging social media platforms like Instagram and LinkedIn can take your real estate network to the next level. By offering value, engaging with your audience, and connecting with others online, you can turn digital interactions into real-world business deals. The power of social media isn't just in posting content—it's in building meaningful relationships that lead to success.

Chapter 7
The Most Important Relationship of All

I can't emphasize enough how crucial it is to have your spouse on board in your real estate business. At some point in your journey—if you haven't already—you'll find yourself in a position where your spouse's support can make or break your success. At AZREIA, during our Launchpad Business Planning sessions, we strongly encourage bringing your spouse along. Even if they won't be directly involved in the business, they need to understand what you're doing, why you're doing it, and the risks involved.

Without that understanding, telling them, "Hey, I'm about to buy this $400,000 house with no roof and no electricity," might make them think you've lost your mind—even if you're sitting on a great deal.

The CPA and the Vision Board

I'll never forget a conversation I had with a new AZREIA member who worked as a CPA at a large firm here in town. We were discussing vision boards and creating clear pictures of our future. I mentioned that I had a vision board hanging in my office, and I looked at it every day. It was right there in front of me as a constant reminder of my goals.

When I asked him where his vision board was, I expected a similar answer—his office, his bathroom, somewhere visible where he could be reminded of his goals every day. Instead, he said, "Oh no, my wife doesn't believe in all that woo-woo stuff." My heart sank when I heard that.

I pressed a little further: "So, where do you keep it?"

He pulled out his wallet and unfolded a tiny piece of paper. As he opened it, the paper kept getting bigger and bigger. "I look at it every day before I walk into work," he said. In that moment, I knew I'd never see him again. His vision, however big it was on that piece of paper, was confined to his wallet—tucked away, hidden, and out of sight. It was clear that without his spouse's support, his dreams would likely stay just that: dreams.

The Power of a Supportive Spouse

On the flip side, I've been fortunate not to have that problem. My wife, Dominique—whom many of you may know from around AZREIA—has always had my back. No matter how crazy my ideas seemed or how uncertain my plans were, she gave me her honest opinion. But most importantly, she supported me fully, even when the path ahead was risky or unclear.

Having a supportive spouse is one of the most powerful assets you'll ever experience. There's nothing else quite like it—except, perhaps, faith. I remember one night in particular, hanging out with friends, when they started asking about how I planned to get started in real estate investing. For people outside the business, flipping houses can sound out of reach or downright crazy.

As I stood behind Dominique, I overheard her say something that still sends chills through my body. She said, "Whatever Mike wants, we get it."

In that moment, I realized it wasn't just about me anymore—it was about us, as a team. That surge of confidence she gave me was something I can't fully explain. But from that moment, I knew nothing could stop me. Her belief in me, in us, gave me a confidence that no deal, amount of money, or business success ever could.

Why This Matters to Your Success

If you're in a relationship, this is hands down the secret sauce to success. It's not just about having someone to back you financially or emotionally—it's about knowing that your spouse believes in your vision, your goals, and your potential. That kind of unwavering support can push you through the toughest challenges.

Your spouse may not be involved in the day-to-day operations of your business, but they are your partner in life, and that partnership must extend to your goals and dreams. Success in real estate often involves taking risks—risks that can feel scary if your spouse isn't on board, understanding and supporting what you're trying to achieve.

Driving the Point Home

You can have the perfect strategy, the best deals, and all the financial know-how in the world, but without your spouse on board, you'll always be fighting an uphill battle. Take the time to involve them in your vision, explain what you're working toward, and build your future together.

As you move forward in your real estate journey, never underestimate the power of this relationship. Just like a great business partnership, the relationship with your spouse is built on trust, communication, and a shared vision. When you're aligned, there's nothing you can't achieve.

Chapter 8
Giving First – A Lifelong Lesson

I first encountered the idea of giving more than receiving when I was just a kid, though I didn't fully understand it at the time. Still, there was something about it that felt right, like an instinct. My grandparents lived in Northeast Philadelphia, and we'd often make the short trip from Connecticut to visit them.

They lived in what were called rowhouses—long, connected townhomes. Philly was always a place full of good memories for me, from the smell of pretzels on the street corners to the comfort of being surrounded by family. But it wasn't the pretzels or the sights of the city that stuck with me most—it was my grandmother's spirit of giving.

Learning to Give: My Grandmother's Lesson

My grandmother came to America from Italy through Ellis Island when she was just seven years old. She became a seamstress in New York City, and that craft stayed with her throughout her life. Her basement was always packed with sewing projects. You couldn't walk down there without shoes unless you wanted to step on a pin or needle, but it wasn't just sewing that kept her busy. My grandmother was always doing something for someone—cooking, lending an ear, or caring for a neighbor in need.

What stood out to me, even as a kid, was that every time someone in the neighborhood passed away, my grandmother would be given something from their estate. And over the years, she was even given two houses. She never asked for these things—people just gave them to her because of the love and care she had poured into the community. But what truly amazed me was when she gave one of the houses away. I didn't understand it at the time, but I see now that she gave selflessly, expecting nothing in return. That spirit of generosity stayed with me, even if I didn't fully realize it back then.

The Law of Reciprocity

Fast forward to my early 20s. I was working as a loan officer, which meant living on commission—if I didn't close deals, I didn't eat. Sales was a game of persuasion, and I was learning how to be better at it every day.

There was a deli downstairs from the office building, and I'd often bump into the owner of the company there. Every time we crossed paths, he'd buy me something—a Red Bull, a sandwich, a pack of gum. It wasn't just a one-time thing. He did it consistently, to the point where I had to ask him, "Why do you always buy me stuff?"

"It's the law of reciprocity," he told me. "Look it up, or read Robert Cialdini's book on persuasion."

So I did. Reciprocity, as I learned, is the practice of exchanging things for mutual benefit. In business and life, it's the idea that if someone does something positive for you, you feel an obligation to return the favor. It's a powerful tool for fostering cooperation and building relationships.

And, of course, it worked. I liked him more, I felt a sense of loyalty, and I wanted to participate in the company culture he was building. But something about it didn't sit right with me. It felt transactional, almost manipulative. He wasn't giving out of kindness or care—he was giving because he expected something in return. The appreciation I had for those small gestures disappeared when I realized that.

I compared that feeling to my grandmother's way of giving. Her generosity was genuine, heartfelt, and never came with strings attached. There was a stark contrast between giving because you care and giving because you want something back.

Give, Give, Give—Then Ask

As my journey in business and sales continued, I came across Gary Vaynerchuk's book Jab, Jab, Jab, Right Hook. Gary's philosophy was different. He taught that you should give, give, give—and only then ask. His approach resonated with me because it was authentic. The "jabs" represented the value you give to your customers or community—your knowledge, your time, your support. And only after you've given enough can you throw the "right hook," asking for something in return.

Gary's message stuck with me, and for the next 10 years, I built my business on this philosophy. I gave value first, and when the time came to ask for a sale or a partnership, it felt fair because I had already earned trust.

AZREIA: Leading Through Giving

When my wife and I took over AZREIA in 2021, I knew we had to continue this strategy. Give, give, give—then ask had gotten me this far, and I knew it could take AZREIA even further. But something changed as I became more involved in the community. I wasn't just hearing about deals anymore—I was hearing the personal stories, the struggles, and the successes of AZREIA members.

People told me about bad characters in the industry, about scams, about their own limitations. Others opened up about how government policies were threatening their businesses. I realized that AZREIA wasn't just a platform for doing deals or selling courses. It was a community, and with that community came a greater responsibility.

I made a decision: From that point forward, I would give with no expectation of getting anything in return. I would wear my heart on my sleeve, offer everything I could, and trust the process. I believed that by doing right by others, God would lead the way.

Since then, you'll never hear me dangle a carrot to get more sales or promise you secret formulas to riches. There's no magic pill or hidden shortcut. I just tell it like it is. And I've learned that giving without expectation isn't always easy—especially when there are bills to pay and responsibilities to meet. But it's the right way to live, and it works.

The Power of Giving Without Expectation

Here's the lesson: Give first. Don't wait for something in return. Don't keep score. Give because it's the right thing to do, because it feels good, and because it builds a foundation of trust and goodwill that no amount of manipulation can create. Whether it's in business, relationships, or community, the more you give, the more you'll find that success follows in unexpected ways.

Taking this approach might feel risky, especially when times are tough. But I can assure you, you won't regret it. Give without expectations—and watch as opportunities you never imagined start to come your way.

Chapter 9

Power Listening: The Key to Building Lasting Relationships

When it comes to building strong relationships, closing deals, or negotiating effectively, there's one skill that stands above the rest: listening. But not just any kind of listening—power listening, the kind that helps you truly understand what the other person is saying, both consciously and unconsciously. As a Master Practitioner of Neuro-Linguistic Programming (NLP), I've seen firsthand how mastering this type of listening can transform interactions and unlock opportunities you might have otherwise missed.

Understanding NLP and Ethical Listening

NLP, or Neuro-Linguistic Programming, is a powerful tool for communication and understanding human behavior. At its core, NLP teaches us how to listen not just to words, but to the deeper layers of communication—body language, tone of voice, and unspoken cues. Through this, we can better understand the emotional and mental states of the people we're interacting with.

Unfortunately, NLP has garnered a bad reputation in some circles, particularly in the dating world, where certain individuals have used it manipulatively. But here's the truth: NLP, when used ethically, is about building trust, understanding, and cooperation. It's about helping people reach their goals, not manipulating them into doing something they don't want to do. The techniques and strategies in NLP should be used to create win-win situations, where both parties benefit from the interaction.

In the world of real estate, this ethical approach is vital. You're dealing with people who are making some of the most significant decisions of their lives—buying or selling a home, investing in properties, or making financial commitments. By using NLP to listen carefully and ethically, you can ensure that you're helping clients make decisions that are truly in their best interest.

The Trap of Self-Focused Listening

One of the biggest barriers to effective listening is our tendency to focus on ourselves during conversations. Often, while someone else is speaking, we're already crafting our response, eager to share our thoughts, solutions, or stories. This habit is not only selfish but also detrimental to building genuine connections.

When we're preoccupied with what we're going to say next, we miss out on crucial information. We overlook the emotions, concerns, and needs that the other person is expressing. In essence, we're not truly listening—we're just waiting for our turn to talk.

This self-focused approach sends a subtle message: What I have to say is more important than what you're saying. It undermines trust and can make the other person feel undervalued or unheard. In contrast, putting the other person first by giving them your full attention fosters respect and strengthens the relationship.

The Power of Listening in Real Estate

When you're talking to a potential buyer, seller, or investor, they're not just giving you information—they're revealing their motivations, fears, and desires. This is where NLP shines. By listening for certain patterns in their language and behavior, you can uncover their real needs, even if they haven't fully articulated them yet.

For instance, in a real estate negotiation, it's common to hear a client say they want a "cozy home with character." While it may seem like a simple preference, it often reflects deeper desires—perhaps a longing for the warmth of a childhood home or a place where they can feel truly themselves. If you're too busy thinking about how to pitch the next property, you might miss these critical cues.

Here's an example: A wife mentions she wants a view of the yard. Instead of just noting it as a checklist item, consider what that view represents to her. Maybe she envisions watching her children play outside or enjoying peaceful mornings with a cup of coffee. By acknowledging and mirroring her desires—saying something like, "I understand that having a beautiful view of the yard where you can watch your kids play is important to you"—you demonstrate that you're truly listening.

This isn't manipulation; it's an example of listening carefully to what matters and responding to it. When people feel heard, they trust you more. They believe that you're looking out for their best interests because you've taken the time to listen deeply. This level of trust is what leads to strong relationships and successful deals.

Active Listening in Practice

When I talk about listening, I don't just mean waiting for your turn to speak. Real listening means being fully present in the conversation, setting aside your own agenda, and immersing yourself in the other person's world.

Here are a few key strategies for becoming a power listener:

Quiet Your Inner Voice: Make a conscious effort to silence the thoughts about what you're going to say next. Focus entirely on the speaker. This takes practice, but it's essential for genuine listening.

Pay Attention to Language Patterns: People tend to express themselves in certain ways—visually, auditorily, or kinesthetically. For example, someone might say, "I see what you're saying," or "That feels right to me." Listen for these cues and use similar language in your responses to create a stronger connection.

Ask Open-Ended Questions: Questions that invite longer, thoughtful responses help you understand what's truly motivating the other person. Instead of asking, "Do you like this property?" ask, "What do you envision your day-to-day life being like in this home?"

Mirror the Other Person: People feel more comfortable with others who are like them. When you subtly mirror someone's body language, tone of voice, or word choice, you make them feel more at ease. But this must be done ethically—genuinely reflecting the way they communicate, rather than trying to manipulate the conversation.

Listen for the Unspoken: Often, what someone doesn't say is just as important as what they do. Watch for shifts in body language or tone that suggest they're hesitant or uncertain, even if their words seem confident. This can give you insight into deeper concerns or fears that they might not be expressing outright.

A Personal Story: Overcoming Self-Focused Listening

Early in my real estate career, I learned a valuable lesson about the importance of putting the other person first. I was meeting with a potential client, Sarah, who was looking to sell her family home after her parents had passed away. I was eager to secure the listing and was mentally preparing my pitch while she spoke.

As Sarah began sharing memories of the home—holidays spent in the living room, her father's garden in the backyard—I realized I was missing important emotional cues because I was too focused on what I would say next. I caught myself and decided to shift my approach.

I set aside my agenda and gave Sarah my full attention. I asked open-ended questions about her experiences and listened without interrupting. She shared her feelings of loss and the difficulty of letting go. By genuinely listening, I was able to understand that this wasn't just a transaction for her; it was a significant emotional milestone.

By the end of our conversation, Sarah thanked me for taking the time to listen. She said she felt heard and understood, which made her comfortable trusting me with the sale of her family home. That experience taught me that when we prioritize the other person's needs over our own desire to speak, we build deeper connections and earn genuine trust.

Listening as a Tool for Trust and Success

The more you listen, the more you can build trust. And in the real estate world, trust is everything. When clients, partners, or colleagues trust you, they're more likely to do business with you, recommend you, and return to you for future deals.

Listening also allows you to create opportunities. By tuning into the subtle cues that others might miss, you can uncover needs and motivations that even your client might not be fully aware of. This gives you the chance to present solutions that others wouldn't think of, giving you a competitive edge.

But perhaps most importantly, listening creates genuine connections. People want to work with those who understand them. When you listen deeply and ethically, you're showing that you value them—not just as a client, but as a person.

Using NLP Ethically in Real Estate

The techniques I've outlined—quieting your inner voice, listening for language patterns, mirroring, and understanding unspoken communication—are all powerful NLP tools. But what makes them truly effective is using them with integrity. Your goal should never be to manipulate someone into doing something that isn't right for them. Instead, it's about creating an environment of trust, understanding, and mutual benefit.

Yes, NLP can be misused. But when applied ethically, it becomes a tool for creating deeper, more authentic relationships. It helps you listen better, understand better, and ultimately, serve your clients better.

In my own experience, the connections I've built through careful, ethical listening have been some of the strongest and most enduring relationships in my career. They've led to more deals, more partnerships, and more opportunities than any sales pitch ever could.

Conclusion

Listening is a skill, but it's also an art. When you master it—when you truly hear people, understand what they're saying, and respond in a way that shows you care—you create something more than just a transaction. You create trust, and with trust comes long-term success.

Remember, every conversation is an opportunity to build a relationship. By putting the other person first and silencing the urge to focus on yourself, you open the door to deeper understanding and meaningful connections. Whether you're negotiating a deal, resolving a conflict, or simply having a conversation, listening is your most powerful tool. And in real estate, it's the difference between being a good agent and a great one.

Conclusion

How One Connection Led to AZREIA

In real estate, success isn't just about numbers or deals—it's about relationships. One connection, one introduction, one moment of trust can change the entire trajectory of your career, and I'm living proof of that.

I first met Stuart at an AZREIA meeting. He was an educator and a local real estate investor, much like myself. We often ran deal scenarios by each other, hoping to make something happen. One day, I came across an off-market condo near the Arizona Cardinals Stadium. It was 2015, and the Super Bowl was heading to Glendale—the Patriots versus the Seahawks. It felt like a golden opportunity.

At the time, I was only four years into the business. I had done a fair amount of wholesaling and maybe had one or two rentals. I wasn't exactly seasoned, but I was learning. I shared the deal with Stuart, and he immediately saw the potential. He wanted to turn it into a short-term rental to capitalize on the Super Bowl rush, and then we'd decide whether to sell or keep it as a long-term rental.

We came up with a plan to buy the property, furnish it, and rent it out for the big game. But then, a serious offer came in that would net me a $6,000 assignment fee. At that point, I hadn't taken down many properties, let alone tried short-term rentals, and frankly, I got cold feet. I decided to sell the deal instead of moving forward with the project.

Stuart was understanding, and we agreed to move on without any hard feelings. But I couldn't shake the feeling that I owed him something. When the deal closed, I decided to cut Stuart a $3,000 check as a token of appreciation. He wasn't expecting it, but I felt it was the right thing to do. That moment turned out to be pivotal.

Stuart spoke highly of me after that, sharing the story of how I paid him, even though he wasn't directly involved in the deal. Without realizing it at the time, I was building trust and a reputation for doing business the right way. Over time, we started working together more, co-hosting networking events, and teaching others the ropes of wholesaling.

That connection with Stuart ultimately led to another life-changing introduction. Stuart was friends with Alan Langston, the founder of AZREIA. He arranged for us to pitch a training program to Alan, but after some discussion, Stuart decided to focus on his own projects. He gave me his blessing to build my own relationship with Alan, and I took it from there.

Alan is a sharp businessman, protective of AZREIA and its members. He doesn't let just anyone into the organization. It took about a year of building trust, back-and-forth emails, and in-person meetings before Alan finally offered me the opportunity to host AZREIA's Beginner Investors Group in 2016. From there, I began teaching classes on raising private money and creative financing strategies.

I learned an important lesson during that time: educate to dominate. When you position yourself as an expert—whether it's through teaching or leading a group—people begin to look to you as a leader. They want to work with you, whether it's partnering on deals, lending money, or seeking guidance.

The Power of Staying in Touch

Let me shift gears for a moment and share another key relationship that made a lasting impact. Remember Aaron, the friend I helped get an internship in New York City at a record label? We stayed in touch over the years, and in 2017, as I continued to grow in real estate, Aaron connected me with Scott, a call center guy who lived between Mexico and Phoenix. Scott had deep connections in the call center world and helped outsource services to American companies.

Through Scott, I started hiring virtual callers for my wholesale business, and it was a game-changer. The benefit of hiring callers from Mexico was that they were in our time zone and spoke fluent English, which gave us a huge advantage over investors hiring from the Philippines. My business grew, and other investors started asking how I was closing more deals.

This sparked a new venture. Scott and I decided to partner up. He provided the call center services, and I brought in clients from the real estate world. We scaled up quickly, growing from a handful of callers to 50 agents, servicing investors and small businesses alike. At our peak, we had 300 employees, all sparked by a connection with Aaron and staying in touch over time.

What made this business unique was how it started small and grew through relationships. Investors would hire three agents at a time, but if they didn't close deals, they'd sometimes disappear, leaving us with agents who were expecting work. That's when we realized we needed an anchor client, a company that could consistently pay and grow with us. Thanks to Scott's relationships in the call center industry, we landed that client.

Here's an inside tip: In the real estate industry, when someone says they "own" a call center, it's usually not true. Most of them outsource their services and white-label it, which is common in many industries. This venture required us to establish ourselves as an official company in Mexico, and at the time of writing this, we have over 300 employees.

All of this came from staying connected with Aaron. While building the wholesale business and the call center with Scott, I was also staying active at AZREIA, continuing my work with the community.

The AZREIA Opportunity

Fast forward to 2021, and Alan approached me about taking over AZREIA. One of the key things we teach at AZREIA is to have a wealth plan, and for Alan, it was time to retire. I was in the perfect position to give back to the community that had helped shape my career, but taking over AZREIA wasn't just an opportunity—it was a significant investment.

That's when I leveraged the real estate principles I had learned. If you recall my Cleveland story, where I wholesaled 25 deals and acquired 10 rental properties, those rentals were all purchased with private funds. I raised 100% of the acquisition and renovation costs through private lenders and their IRAs, with no money out of my pocket.

Now, I decided to sell those properties, using the profits to take on this new opportunity. Just like in Monopoly, where you trade four greenhouses for one red hotel, I leveraged those deals to buy into AZREIA—the largest real estate investment association in the country.

Full Circle

So here we are, back to where it all began: Stuart. This entire journey—the wholesale deals, the call center business, taking over AZREIA—started with one connection in 2014. Two guys just trying to put some deals together.

Never underestimate anyone. Never disregard any relationship. Treat everyone with respect and always have the intention to build, without expecting anything in return. I like to say, "For every dud, there's a stud." You never know where your next big opportunity will come from. Sometimes, it leads to something bigger than you ever could have imagined.

And that's the power of fearless connections.

Fearless Connections as a Framework

Throughout this book, I've shared stories, insights, and lessons that highlight the power of building relationships that go beyond transactional networking. These are Fearless Connections—authentic, intentional relationships that help you achieve long-term success. Now, it's time to bring everything together into a framework you can use as you build your real estate career or any business that thrives on human connections.

Giving First

Always offer value before asking for something in return. Whether it's advice, support, or connections, leading with generosity builds trust and opens doors. Remember, the connections you nurture today will pay off in ways you might not even expect. By giving without expectation, you create a foundation of trust, which is the most valuable currency in any business.

Building with Rising Stars

Seek out those who are hungry for success and grow alongside them. Some of the most rewarding partnerships come from people who are still in the early stages of their journey. These are the people who are eager to learn, collaborate, and innovate. As they rise, so do you. Nurturing relationships with driven individuals keeps your network vibrant and full of fresh opportunities.

Mastering the Follow-Up

Consistency is key. Real connections aren't made in a single meeting or through one email. They're built over time through persistent, thoughtful follow-up. Following up demonstrates reliability and a genuine interest in the relationship. Never underestimate the power of a well-timed follow-up message to keep relationships alive and growing. This step is crucial in moving beyond an introduction to building lasting connections.

Leveraging Online and In-Person Networking

Whether it's on social media or at a local meetup, always show up and engage with others. Social media can be an invaluable tool for building relationships at scale, but don't forget the value of in-person connections. Use both strategically to expand your network. A balanced approach of virtual and face-to-face engagement ensures that you remain accessible and connected in a meaningful way.

Growing Together

As you build your network, recognize the value of growing alongside the people you connect with. When you help others succeed, you're creating a community of partners who are invested in each other's success. Over time, this collective growth multiplies your opportunities and impact. A growing, thriving network is one of your most valuable business assets, and when you invest in the growth of others, you guarantee mutual success.

Fearless Connections in Action

At its core, Fearless Connections is about relationships. It's not about taking shortcuts or building shallow, transactional connections. It's about nurturing authentic relationships that stand the test of time. Whether you're at the beginning of your journey or well on your way, this framework will serve as the foundation for building trust, earning respect, and unlocking opportunities.

As you move forward, remember: the real magic of Fearless Connections lies in consistency and authenticity. Be patient, give without expecting anything in return, and watch as your network blossoms into something much bigger than yourself.

Your Next Step

The Call to Action

You've read the stories, learned the lessons, and seen the framework. Now, it's time for action. Building a successful real estate business—or any business—doesn't happen in isolation. It happens through connections. And now is the time for you to start building your own Fearless Connections.

Here's what you can do right now to take the next step:

Join the AZREIA Community at: AZREIA.org/join

If you haven't already, I encourage you to join AZREIA. We're more than just a real estate investment group—we're a community of like-minded individuals working together to help each other succeed. Take advantage of the resources, networking opportunities, and the vast pool of knowledge within AZREIA.

Sign up for our monthly meetings

These gatherings are the perfect place to start building your own network. Whether you're new to the industry or an experienced investor, there's always something to learn and someone to connect with.

Participate in workshops and online events

AZREIA offers a variety of educational workshops designed to help you sharpen your skills, from deal analysis to raising capital. Dive in, learn, and connect with others who are on the same path.

Engage in our online forums

Connect with other investors, ask questions, share insights, and form partnerships that will help you grow your business. Leverage these forums as a space to collaborate, learn, and grow with fellow investors.

Start Giving Before You Ask

Begin practicing the Fearless Connections framework today. Reach out to someone in your network with no agenda other than to offer value. Whether it's sharing a lead, giving advice, or just being a sounding board, the more you give, the stronger your connections will become.

Build Your Online Presence

Don't underestimate the power of social media in building your network. Start by sharing your journey, offering value, and engaging with others in the industry. Whether it's LinkedIn, Instagram, or Facebook, the relationships you start online can lead to powerful partnerships in the real world.

Master the Follow-Up

Take a look at your current network and identify a few key people you haven't connected with recently. Send them a thoughtful message to re-engage. Consistent follow-up is one of the most powerful tools for maintaining and strengthening your relationships.

Conclusion: Fearless Connections and Your Future

The future of your real estate journey—or any business endeavor—hinges on your ability to build lasting, meaningful relationships. Fearless Connections isn't just a framework for networking; it's a way of living and doing business that puts trust, generosity, and mutual success at the forefront.

So, go out there and start building your network with intention. Be fearless, give before you ask, and watch as your connections grow into lifelong partnerships. The opportunities are limitless when you make Fearless Connections the foundation of your business and your life.

Remember, AZREIA is here to support you every step of the way. Tap into the resources, the community, and the wisdom we've built, and let's grow together.

About the Author

Michael Del Prete is a seasoned real estate investor, entrepreneur, and the Executive Director of the Arizona Real Estate Investors Association (AZREIA), the largest REIA in the nation. With over a decade of hands-on experience, Michael has successfully completed more than 700 real estate transactions, including building a diverse rental portfolio. Alongside his wife, Dominique, he co-founded We Heart Houses, a company that specializes in creative real estate investment solutions.

Renowned for his leadership and vision, Michael has empowered thousands of investors to thrive in the competitive real estate market by providing top-tier education, resources, and networking through AZREIA. He also co-hosts The AZREIA Show podcast, where he shares expert insights on real estate strategies, wealth-building, and the latest industry trends.

Beyond his professional achievements, Michael is a devoted family man. He and his wife, Dominique, share their journey with their son, Diego. As a frequent speaker at real estate conferences nationwide, Michael emphasizes the importance of building meaningful connections and leading with value—principles that have defined both his personal and professional life.

About Arizona Real Estate Investors Association

AZREIA is a nationally recognized and award-winning trade association. Our success is due to our members' commitment to our organization. In return, we provide valuable resources, proven strategies, and timely market updates that help our members achieve their real estate investment goals.

AZREIA's purpose is to unlock and accelerate our members ability to invest in real estate through education, market information, support, and networking opportunities so that they can elevate their financial well-being.

We offer Association Meetings every month where you have access to the latest investment information, business associates who understand your needs, and a great networking environment. There are classes, workshops, and investing seminars which provide you the education and training to increase your ability to be successful, networking resources to help you build a team of advisors and business associates, easy access to experts in all areas of real estate investment, small sub-groups of members with similar investment interests, online forums to help you market your properties or services to other investors and ask questions, support and motivation to be successful in the exciting and profitable area of real estate investing, and discounts from national vendors and local Business Associates to save you money and time.

How AZREIA will help you achieve your goals:

1. **Education** - Education is important, but it isn't everything. Focusing your education on areas that will help you achieve your objectives is what's important. AZREIA offers in-house education in most key areas of real estate investing and access to the most credible national educators. An important first step is to take the Core Skills workshops.

2. **Building Your Team** - AZREIA has a Business Associate Program with virtually all the services and products you will need fully represented. Save months by establishing relationships with these companies who understand your needs and recognize you are unique.

3. **Controlling Your Cost & Saving Money** - AZREIA members have access to exclusive benefits from dozens of our Business Associates and major national companies like The Home Depot where our members receive a 2% rebate and exclusive pricing on paint and appliances. AZREIA members, on average, save over $1000/year each through our expansive relationships.

4. **Market Information** - As you become experienced, the in-depth Market Update is a relied upon resource to assist in adjusting your investing to current market conditions. The knowledge you gain from this valuable tool will help you communicate effectively with potential sellers, buyers, and investors. The Market Update is invaluable and free to members.

5. **Community** - AZREIA is a community of thousands of members across the state of Arizona. We have several groups that meet monthly to help build strong relationships between members. Many of our members have found business partners, deals, and even friends within the community that help empower each other and hold each other accountable. Our meetings and events help bring real

estate investors together to create more meaningful relationships throughout their investing journey.

Membership with AZREIA gives you massive discounts on education, resources, and other opportunities. Plus, you have access to meet thousands of investors across the state! The Plus membership gives you all-inclusive access to our meetings for those highly active investors that come to our meetings often. Standard membership lets you pay as you go, choosing when you can attend during your busy schedule! Both memberships give you the same access to the local and national discounts, our forums, and other great investor resources. The savings are HUGE!

AZREIA's Monthly Meetings are always packed with investors!

We would love for you to join in on our mission, if it aligns with yours, to educate those in your family, community, and state about financial literacy and freedom through real estate investing.

Our Membership Guarantee is that we will provide you the smartest and most reliable path to achieve success in real estate investing through impactful networking, quality information, premium education, and a thriving community. If you're interested in joining our vision, get in touch with us in any of the following ways:

Email: MemberServices@azreia.org

Phone: 480-990-7092

Web: azreia.org

Address: 4527 N 16th St #105, Phoenix AZ 85016

Facebook: @azreia

Instagram: @arizona_reia

YouTube: @azreia

TikTok: @arizonareia

AZREIA's Fix & Flip Bus Tour with The Home Depot

NOTES:

NOTES:

Made in the USA
Columbia, SC
05 November 2024